Thumbsucker

poems

Kat

Giordano

Published by Malarkey Books

Cover design: Angelo Maneage

ISBN: 979-8-9874654-2-4

Kat Giordano's *Thumbsucker* is one of those bruised, bloody-knuckled, cut-lipped books that has flung itself into life and all its suffering and is here to tell you, dripping in manna and umbra, how it survived. But behind this, cast like a shadow at dusk, is an argument that says despite its pain, its ugliness, life is beauty, is splendor, laughter and love. Read these poems for the iron in them, for Giordano's ability to rock you with a line like a surprise left hook. Return for the way these poems part the dark to show you something bright. "it felt wrong of me / to eulogize something I killed, / to miss it, even, / and still not be sorry."

—Todd Dillard, author of *Ways We Vanish*

While reading *Thumbsucker* I thought of my grandfather, who cut off the tip of his ring finger with a circular saw. These poems are instruments so perfectly sharp, spinning at such a merciless speed, that when they cleanly separate you from yourself, all you can do is smile manically and wait for the pain to come.

—William Duryea, Editor in Chief of *Misery Tourism*

In *Thumbsucker*, the dingy dive bars, ex-loves, and junior high bullies of Kat Giordano's life are portals to unexpected worlds. These poems are emotional snapshots of despair; no matter how blinding a light once was, the images always fade.

—Graham Irvin, author of *I Have A Gun*

Kat Giordano has written a collection that is so real and specific it might as well be your own memories. These poems puked all over my heart. These poems put their fingers in my mouth and I liked it.

—Axel B. Kolcow, Deputy Editor of *Taco Bell Quarterly*

No wolf seems to wanna end up
On the same note as any other in the choir
This is why a dog howling along
With a group of singing humans is instantaneously noticeable
He is deliberately not in the same register as the other voices
And seems to revel in the discordant sound he is making
He thrives in his own decadence
He bathes in his own dirt
He does not conform to what society believes is best for him
He doesn't need to be Best In Show because it's his show
It's his party and he can kick, and scream, and cry if he wants to
He belongs not to the Earth, but the Earth belongs to him
He is unique, he is an individual, he is alone
(He is alone)

—"Best In Show II," Viagra Boys

REAL ART

I don't know what you people want,
though it's probably the exact opposite
of this poem. turduckened
self-pity. this anemic, sad-girl
whining. illegal, off-script
survey card slipping under the door
of whatever makeshift dad
I've made up today.

don't tell anyone about me
breathing into your DMs like
i Showed u my poem,, anwser me
and I won't tell anyone
what you said back.

we all need a place
to uncork our longings. our screeds
they try and relegate to diaries.

the part of me that's always sitting
in an armchair, drinking a 40
with its belly out, waiting for you
to leave the room so it can fart
without having to make a joke
or say something useful.

the part of you that just wants
to undress for once without stepping
into something more comfortable,
without pretending you wake up
that way, not terrified it's just you
under all the tulle and wiring.

I've done that myself, peeled the skin
off the bones, and what I bled
was still just blood.

can't tell you how many times
I've pulled out all the stops for you
just to trip over them.

LOVE POEM

for 22 years of my life,
I got nothing out of sunsets.

I never knew what to do or feel in church
or during SPCA commercials,
what I was supposed to look at
when we "took a drive"
on all those beach vacations.

all of those clickbait stories—
dead dogs and army dads
and public prom-posals—
ricocheted off me
like cheap, plastic darts.

even in college,
the entirety of canonized poetry
piled like pale yellow kernels
I pushed around my plate.

nobody knew this about me,
I didn't know it,
I was a writer. I said "beautiful"
at all of the right times,
the ones prescribed to me
by Twitter and Culture and Art,
but I don't remember a time
before you
where my soul twitched or swelled
or ached, even once.

I was a flaccid bag
of Kraft mac n cheese
waiting to use the computer.

I related to nothing
but my own poison guts.

now, the notes of certain songs
bruise and inflame me the whole way down,
gag me on my blood.
I tear up at commercials with babies.
cloudy days make me sad.

I worry I'll wake up
and my brain will be back
to its old one-note static,
the bloodless gray creeping in the corners
of every cornfield we watch.

ARS POETICA III

maybe it was because I'd chugged
half a bottle of wine back at the hotel
before we left. wine still altered things
back then, shaved down the bones
and made it all charming, harmless,
candy-red velvet. those days I thought
would somehow be the last
of the bad ones, before grad school,
that last-ditch letter I still believed
was coming. it was an offsite reading
upstairs above a jazz club. a few
miles away, the worst possible man
had just taken the worst possible office
and the city was a vacuum
of us all waiting for the first bad thing
to happen. it was there, too,
in the jazz club attic, the soft murmurs
before the set, all of us pretending
we'd know something pure if we heard it.
and her at that mic, trying her best
to say some perfect thing, the trying
its own weird relief. in the Uber
on the way back I held myself
with this practiced reverence, desperately
moved, like watching a body cut open,
noting the frayed-out edge of the wound
and willing one flimsy stitch to hold.
I got home later that week and found

a skinny envelope. grad school
didn't want me. and we all know
what happens later: the vacuum stops
and the worst possible man still won't
and I still keep trying to have
a religious experience. and watch
each stomach as it's cut open.
and hold that shaky needle in my hand
convinced that there's something noble
in the threading.

DM ME YOUR ADDRES

spent tonight taping cards and letters
up on the wall behind my desk
to avoid working:
a nice note from an editor
with a sunflower seal.
christmas card from a friend
whose wedding I should have gone to
but was too depressed to show up.
the logo of a friend's old press,
hovering beside them in groovy, black font.

I like touching things my friends have touched,
like to picture their hands, stoned and fumbling
with a pen and a piece of cardstock,
thinking of me while they write my name.
a person I've never seen
sitting in some room I've never been in,
aiming paper airplanes at my desk
where I'll later hang them crookedly,
catching strands of my hair in the tape.

I like seeing strands of my hair touching
things my friends have touched.

something to look at while I'm working,
on those days where I swear
if I have to write another 4,000 words
about "cognitive analytics"
I'll scrape my entire brain out of my ear
with one of my tiny green paperclips.

those days I wake up and think,
"by the end of the day
I'll have gotten all of this done,"
and then all of a sudden the day is over
and I haven't gotten all of it done,
and I realize that it's been so long
since I've sat on the beach with a friend,
and all the bands I loved in college
keep releasing albums
about how all of the good times
already happened.

those days all I can do is pray
that it's really true, that thing they say
about the heart being a muscle,
and that one day, mine will bend my ribs
with its bare hands and come strutting out,
all oiled-up and veiny,
with the beefiest fucking calves.

and when that day finally comes
I'll mail signed vanity shots
to every single one of my Twitter friends
and be like, "it's just like that thing they say!!"
and they'll be like, "holy shit!"

HIGH SCHOOL REUNION

you have half a beard now, and I'm gassy
and sweat-soaked under three pounds of makeup.
we look like a running gag in the first episode
of a 90s sitcom reboot.

I go up to hug you and I swear
the whole group scatters around us,
probably expecting me to start up some blowout
or throw a drink on your head, which I don't
because I still need them to think I'm cool,

and because as we're sipping on cheap beer,
bullshitting about your job and my book,
I can feel you begging me
not to say it—

how I cried for weeks over you
and you called me an Anorexic Stalker Chicken
in my eighth-grade yearbook. the almosts,
how you diced me with your eyes
and let me sweat there for a decade,
cook down into something even less
than a girl. the small part of me
craving your silence, though it lives on
in every unliked photo and unanswered text
and my boyfriend's stillness
while he sits smoking at the edge of our bed—
how I'm doomed to transpose you
onto the face of every well-meaning person
who's done nothing wrong.

tonight, you touch my shoulder and joke
that I probably kept all our AIM chat logs,
and I laugh instead of telling you to go fuck yourself.
I tell you I'm in therapy and don't say
how much is your fault.
I smoke your joint in the rain,
shield my damp hair with my jacket
like you're not still the anvil I cower under,
bare my pale arms beneath the streetlight and pretend
the scars don't sting when the light hits them.

I AM NOT A CROOK

I'm scared I'm the only one here
who knows what anything means,

not like an arcane text but the only cat
in a roomful of humans meowing.

my tears look so stupid
when they don't hear the high-pitched whine
their words make scraped
against their actions.

I'm the baby they want to toss
off the wing of the plane
with my nonsensical wailing

and I can't explain my head
is too small

face-down, bloodied,
crying on a tarmac
as a clown-car plane of Nixons
struts out, throwing up V's.

THUMBSUCKER POEM

fuck me I guess but I want everything
soft and full of kittens. I want
to step out and romp to the car
on cushy, pink clouds. that feeling
of late afternoon on a Friday
my freshman year of college—eating oreos
while the older guys left to buy beer—
bottled, sugared, delivered to me daily
by a puppy in a bright red bandana.

I want that look I know I'd get
if I started seizing in the middle of Walmart
but for no reason, a halo of faces
that just want to help, dripping with concern
as they piece together the plan. a eulogy
minus death, plus balloons.

I miss getting stickers.
I miss second-grade sick days
and people running when I scraped my knees.

I'm not convinced I'm damaged
to miss these things. I felt damaged
in the city, when I'd come home at night
tired, oily, all covered in the world—
coughing, car horns, my building's super
calling another guy a cunt on the sidewalk.
I prefer to believe there's somewhere better
I was meant to be born,

some gummy thumbsucker world,
a quilted, trashless warmth
that lasts forever,
where there's always a hug when you need it.

when I was little, my mom would enter my room
and turn a key in the butt of a little stuffed sheep
that played "you are my sunshine"
over and over, slower and slower
'til it would stop
and I'd lie there the whole time
frozen in fear in the dark
as the song petered out, wanting to cry
at how temporary it was.

TO THE RUST BELT, WITH LOVE
for J.

you finish your gig at the bar
reading poems about the bar
you ducked into last month
after another gig at the bar
reading poems about it.

in Missouri, in Ohio, in Pennsylvania,
you drink a whiskey that tastes like a whiskey
you once wrote a poem about remembering.

that's how everything is, now
at the end of the poem
about the end of America: a beaten horse
liquifying in your mouth.

in every whiskey,
the memory of better whiskey.
in every bar,
the memory of a better bar,
the one where you asked the too-thin woman her
name
and she told you, and her hand on your shoulder
became the poem you've been writing ever since.

it's a dream you have
while driving, and you've been driving
for a very long time, passing ghosts
of your own car as I-76 swallows itself.
you think if you can somehow get off

this loop, there's a dive
waiting there, pure and lore-less,
a gas ball at the beginning of time,
or memory, and inside, the first girl
will be sitting there,
drinking a whiskey,
waiting for you to show up.

IT'S ALRIGHT

I crossed the desert just to tell you
I crossed the desert.

for years,
lugging this stone on my back
just to tell you its weight.

I could've not.
I could've called you.
I could've found a hillside
and skipped down
and seen you there, waving,
from across a big lake.

I could've set the rock down,
collapsed, and let the sun cook me
and you'd be a jackal
sniffing my body.

I could've seen a white flower
and eaten it, and the sky
would fill with fractals of your face.

I could've touched my hand
and realized it was your hand, too,
and kissed it.
we're alone,
and the clothes I lay at your feet
are bone-stiff, salted with sweat.

it doesn't make this more beautiful.
they're just there, stinking,
and my back is bruised.

I know,
but don't say it.

I know,
but I'm tired,
and I need you,
and my feet are cracked.

just let me lay here.
let me just lay.

I'll tell you the story
while you comb out my hair
in the dark.

FOR A FRIEND, IN LIEU OF A REHAB LETTER
for C.

it sucks shit trying
to make a new life.
I've done it before
and it wasn't my favorite.

I hated every second
trapped in the first act,
my whole life piled
in my arms, impossible
to know, conversations
amounting to nothing.

could have jerked off
to the thought
of an inside joke.

lurid fantasies
of collective lore,
someone seeing a mug
in a Target and knowing
it's something I'd like.

I walked so long
in that silence, talking
the whole time.
then you came, and I was

rooted. not right away,
but a little, enough
for the cracks to fill,
for me to see you weren't
alone in that slow swell
into something like family
when I'm squinting,
then all the time.

what I'm saying is
you don't have to
do it all right now.
hang out awhile
and you'll lose it
like a bad cough.

a new tooth in the gap
you've been running
your tongue over,

a thin ring thawed
around the light.

CREATION MYTH

when I was young
I swallowed a cone of light.
my stomach hurt and everyone said
I was lying.

the rest is history. you know,

like a dog who swallowed a small toy,
got into the glitter.
you have to bend and pick out
the little bits glimmering
in the shit.

every year feels like seven,
and I only know a few words,
and I only know them in
certain tones.

you don't know why
I do many things.

why a noise can be enough
to make me dart off
to the edge of the yard
and stand there all night, looking.

I'm afraid the light will run out
and it will be like dying.
I'm afraid of how small I want to be,
of what passes, now, for control.

like a cartoon doing science,
pulling a lever so hard it breaks off
and the machine runs forever.

I will now walk to the store
in a tight little shirt.
I will be a blurred cutout
in the background of some man
buying coffee, and if he talks to me
I will say what anyone else would say
at a time like this.

I will pretend to be a person
who is not so great,
and I will pretend to be pretending.

UNTITLED

I only seem to open
when challenged,
when I can prove something.

you think I'm hard,
so I want to be tender,
a lava cake cracked
and pooling around you,
or an egg un-boiling.

only under tension,
when I'm bitten into.

when the last thing you want
is writhing, white-hot surrender.

you're available.
this is not about being available.
in my dreams, you crank
our little pain machine,
smiling like the devil.

I built it and you
just work there.
it's cold at night,
when you're home,
when you've shut it down.
I take up talking to myself.

I build castles for people
who already live someplace.
castles I could have built others.

castles I could have built myself.

ON SECOND THOUGHT...

for a moment there
I was in bed and nothing
in the phone felt real to me.

I thought, I could
never hear from him again
and be fine. one breath
and he'll pass through
my body like a shudder,
quick as he came.

then I'll really be living.

I'll sleep on time,
dream only of dogs,
being in high school,
people I actually know.

I'll sit in rooms
and really be in them,
feel each atom of air.

sexless, quiet.

I won't lie there
and picture a man watching
in the corner, Cullen-like,
while I tense my legs.
when I die, they'll remember

my air of mystery:
"someone everyone knew,"
they'll say, "but no one
knew well." it was him,
after all, that made me open,
a torrent of verbal diarrhea
each time I had a new worry
or thought. one breath,
and we can kill poetry.
I can sit here, restrained,
polish my inner life
like a bronze peacock,
place it out of the way,
finally, to watch the room.

I inhale, and hold it—

ANNA

Anna was so pretty she took selfies
the way most people check email.
any time, she could angle her phone down,
click once, and capture something
in the upper tier of human. meanwhile
I would sit there for all two hours
of the best light in our bedroom
just to get one of her outtakes.

holy fuck, was I jealous.
her not-big, not-small, nothing nose,
her red curls wild and not. no friends,
I'd sit at the edge of my bed on fridays
while she painted her pout
skittle-red in the mirror, close-reading
men's texts for her while she slipped on
her tight black onesies and boots,
and I'd stare dumbly when she said
things like, "does this look slutty?"
feeling gawky and small
and lucky to be asked.

weekday mornings Anna interned,
PR or something, at the mall,
and I'd squint awake to Elle King
and her blow dryer, and I'd hit snooze
between frames of her shrugging on blazers
in every color but black.
she left every room in body mist

and the fading jingle of her bracelets
and my heart hurt.

like somebody's mom
when I was still young enough
to find moms wise and cool,
she seemed to know things
about looking grown-up and beautiful,
some innate wisdom I'd never learned
and was too old to be taught.

but that was all my secret.

in the room with her, I'd peel my towel off
like nothing, do my eyebrows badly,
air-dry in the open by the first-floor window
like I was the same.
like I wasn't the nerd girl in a movie
before she takes her ponytail down
and her glasses off.

then she'd leave,
and I'd make myself late for class
taking 40 ugly pictures with her pout
and using her flat iron.

DUDES

dudes are everywhere.

dudes are at your job
and on your bus and in front of you
in line at Six Flags
grabbing their girlfriend's ass.

you walk down the street and it's dude street,
dude words hurled out of dude cars at stoplights
as you weave through dudes in dude suits
and dude dogs piss on sidewalks.

dude jobs
dude songs
dude books
dude jabs and grabs and jokes

don't get me started on what happens
in bars. what escape is there but lying
in the tub with wine and scraping
all the dude you can
off your body?

you go on the internet
and there are dudes on the internet
and the internet can't fathom
containing anything, anyone
but dudes. these dude-shaped
holes are the name of the game

and you kill yourself trying
to bend through them.

if you're good
it's a fun performance,
how they redden when you lift up
your soles to your ears

and if you're not,
it's sad, lonely bruises.

you might wonder if dudes ever get bored
of themselves, picture other worlds
awash in brand-new, non-dude oceans

but to dudes,
dudes are not dudes,
and the water is water. they stare through
their laser-cut outlines in the wall, pouting,
and motion you in.

FIGHTING OVER THE PIANO
for A.

self-taught, he moved
like his hands were missing bones,

rubbing up against
the limits of my knowledge,
the rigid shapes I'd perfected
through years of lessons,
reams of gold-star stickers
in song books, those goddamn
mnemonic devices...

Every Good Boy Does Fine,
but it's a problem.
you never hear a grace note,
nothing coils up inside you
like a clef around the G.

I suddenly started to hate
all that I'd learned.

now, I wanted him
to put me in a blindfold, force me
to make new shapes with my hands.

ALONE WITH EVERYBODY

I was 22, and for the first time
I knew no one at the party

my friends had bailed,
and I just stood there, obscure
at the periphery of beer pong
with the smokers,
laughing when they laughed.

sometimes I'd bend to pick up a ball
that had rolled between my feet.
some guy would thank me
and I'd flinch when our hands met
in the handing-off.

it was kind of quiet there,
in the basement. with the door shut
you could barely hear the music,
the party up above a kind of mass
that swelled and settled
as the ceiling groaned under its weight.

down here it splintered off
into pockets of gossip
and aimless flirting. taken
under the wing of some girl
to a ring of friends riffing
on someone I'd never meet,

I stood darting my eyes
between their faces, searching
for ways around
the velvet rope of their grins.

they'd split to piss and come back
with dispatches from the field:
a pizza lost in transit.
Ryan's Girlfriend.
some freshman passed out
hunched over the toilet and
when you walked in
you could hear his wet snores
echo off the bowl.

laughing at the right times, looping
all the right animations,
trying not to burp.

maybe the next joke will crack it open
and I'll slide in,
the perfect size for that space.
I'll say something
that everyone will laugh at
and they'll lift me up
on wings of their acceptance,
up the stairs, out the door,
untouchable
and bathing in their light.
at 1 AM the beer was gone
and the basement near-empty.
two guys calling a ride,
another asleep in a lawn chair.

I wove past the stragglers and upstairs
trying to get un-marooned.
everyone left was on the couch
binging Vine compilations
to run out the clock.
it was a cuddle pile—
too much red tape.

I ordered the Uber
and waited out front, where Toilet Boy
was being coaxed back to life by his friends.
hey man do you want water? hey,
run in and get him some water,
make sure he has water.
alright buddy, just a little more
and once we get in the car
you're golden. is he
going with you? yeah,
he can sleep on my couch.
you're gonna be fine, buddy.

as I listened I pictured myself
passing out on the curb
and dying alone and friendless
in my own puke.

I spoke my first word all night
passing Toilet Boy to get to the car.
surfacing from between his own knees
with half-lidded eyes, he slurred,
"you've got a blood stain on your ass,"
and I said, "thanks."

PLAYING THE HITS

tonight I've been playing the hits.

maybe it's the burger I ate
or the unseasonable cold,

and I know right now I sound
like those poetry guys I make fun of,
but tonight when I close my eyes
there's that little red car
with the backseats all packed full of booze
and it's right and well-rendered
and rotating inside my mind.

the dry evening chill and warm burgers
in thin, greasy foil.

that little house where we'd chug beers
and spin Folk of the 80s
and the lights were always coiled
around the bannister.

I once got so high, I thought
you were crying, that you'd turned
to look at me and realized
I was the most beautiful thing
you'd ever seen, and it made you weep
because we couldn't be together,
because this was always going to end.
it's Saturday, summer—

in another life we're stumbling
all tripped-out on the bayfront,
dodging invisible lights,
the rent-a-cops walking like hexagons.

sometimes, late at night
I think so, so hard
and I don't even know
what I'm thinking about.

it's odd,
and then I remember.

DRIVING WITH JASON

started to make me uncomfortable.
not for the reasons you think, though,
not because he was twice my age
or how he looked at me at stoplights.
not getting breakfast together on Sundays,
what people must have thought
of me beside him in a diner, beaming
and wearing a big flannel.
their assumptions mattered little to me,
they weren't my business,
maybe it made him feel good
to have me there, young
and dumb enough,
but that didn't matter, either.

we were even in my bed once,
nothing weird happened,
we watched Princess Mononoke, we hugged
goodbye at the door, I curled back
in my blankets, heard the elevator
slither past me in the wall.

but he understood too much,
too much was the same,
too much in his eyes.
face-to-face in those bars
I almost couldn't do it.
I'd never known someone over 40
with eyes like that, still sad and wet,

no crust on them.
when I imagined myself at that age,
those eyes were not a possibility.
I'd have the eyes of a snake
or a worn toy plush,
these hard, knowing marbles.
I didn't want to think about being
that old with those eyes, that old
with no callouses, still getting drunk
with near-strangers in cemeteries
and falling asleep in my jeans.

on Superbowl Sunday, we got Waffle House
and he drove us to Morgantown
the long way—joints in the glove box,
passenger-seat paper-bag whiskey,
mountain curves so sharp
even he got lost. I picked the music,
it was Mitski the whole way down.

then, an hour from home,
sitting in the Mexican restaurant,
my newly-exed boyfriend texted
to insist I had made a mistake,
asking to talk things over.

Jason went to the bathroom and came back
without advice. he watched me stare
into my drink as it watered down.
in the car, I ranted in circles,
he said things like, "that's how it goes,"
and then dropped me off.

in bed that night, I wanted nothing
more than comfort, but I knew then
what I wanted was impossible. after that,
Jason and I didn't go any farther
than Butler County, and one day
he stopped picking me up.

AMY WITH THE HIGH VOICE

the guy who broke my heart in middle school
now sends me thirst texts whenever I'm in town.
he always starts out friendly,
has the courtesy to ask how I've been before revealing
he's drunk and horny and, occasionally, sorry
for writing that I look like the chicken from *Chicken Run*
in my eighth-grade yearbook, which really means
he wishes he'd known I'd turn out pretty. back then

he was chasing after Amy With The High Voice
whose handwriting looked like perfect 8 pt. Arial.
I once got my hands on a note she gave him
and filled entire pages trying to mimic her flawless script,
'til "*i love you* ♥" was a kind of science, less painful
than the words. I had an end-of-school-year party
the week after she broke his heart. he showed up
guitar in hand, and under the still-setting sun
I sat pretzel-style in the grass, watching
his long fingers flex as he strummed. the lyrics
were about her but I wouldn't hear them,
open-mouthed, panting, mosquito-venom drunk.

that same summer, he said he tried to like me back
but just couldn't see me as a girl. I'm on
his side of the script now, ghosting
at the part when he says how bad he wants me.
but I still tense up hard writing my a's, try to master
that perfect loop, that dainty, font-like restraint.

TRACING THE HOLE

I look at your Instagram and pretend
I'm still friends with you,
pawing through photos like I'll absorb
your fun by osmosis—the deep exhale
of a friday night, a half-dozen hugs
in that living room with everyone waiting.

the same sameness I once cupped in my hands
and wrung out, like a rodent
or a large orange. that spring
I kept posting these love notes
to freedom, flat alibis
for the wet rinds in my palms.

it felt wrong of me
to eulogize something I killed,
to miss it, even,
and still not be sorry.

it still does,
but you're far away enough now
that i can say these things,
trace the hole I left
without being sucked back.

your new roommate and I
have the same first name.
I wonder if you still have to specify
when you say it in stories.

LIGHT MAGIC

funny how the best person out there
is always the one I happen to
know. my favorite trick of the light.

I think it's actually the light
I love so much. or, gesturing
so the cameraman pans to center me,
my light. my pet that slithers
into bed with me, requests
I ricochet if off things, surfaces, you
being one such surface.

that is how I will explain this
to the reader, the friends who wonder
why I'm doing this again, tying
my own hands behind my back and throating
the knife. can't be the mark
if I'm in on the trick. can't
be your pet if I'm the one
with the pet, the one doing
the petting. need I remind you
it's the light, not me, bouncing
off you, nobody bruising.

that's why this doesn't hurt
and couldn't be wrong, why I could
reach behind your ear right now
and pull out a coin, a dove, a handful
of small, silver stars.

the master of ceremonies,
bending light beams with a whip
and a kitchen chair, nothing here
I cannot control. if you stick around

you'll get the big reveal,
the main attraction, the one
they come from out of town for:
I say, "just today I found the best person
there ever was and ever will be,"
then I lift a big tarp
to reveal that the best person out there
is the one I happen to know
and nobody has ever figured out
how the fuck I keep doing it.

THE LAST OF US EPISODE 3

well, here I am again.
saw something beautiful on TV
and now it's everyone's problem,

especially yours, for the messages
I'll leave you while you're sleeping,
increasingly crazed, sopping
with honey and blood:

"the devil made you
in some kind of factory."

"I want you to cuff me
to a fence somewhere,
like an abandoned dog."

"would you kill me
if I asked you to?

would you cry?"

you won't know how I sat on the bed tonight,
frothing at the men on the screen
while they fucked and fought, their grunts
passing through me like weather.

if only I were a man
and you were the type
to find this kind of thing arresting,

or to ask me, on nights like these,
what I'm thinking about.

right now, I'm thinking
the price of love
is never being boring again,
never having a thought
that isn't dragging the whole world with it
screaming, by the scruff.
some might say that's the joy in it—

A SECRET THIRD THING

holy fuck I feel alive
and like lying to myself
about things that don't matter.

I have a driver's license. I floss
twice a day. I have never
felt this way before. it has never
ended poorly and the blood is fake,
cornstarch and Ehlers red pooling
in my nail beds, piano keys.
there's more where that came from.

...

I want to ask you
if I can ask you a question
and then not actually ask it,

in your mind like a Cheshire cat
grinning through red fire.

I kneel between your feet
and you rip lightning
out of my throat.

...

none of this
is important.
still, it's a feat
anytime you move the heavens
and earth, even a few inches,
enough to bump your hip
on new corners, think twice
putting your foot down.

now my heartbeat's in time
and everyone else is wrong.

sure, it's lonely...

...

in the blue evening
my dog leaps up,
front paws on the fence,
staring at people a street away
with her ears back,
not guarding or friendly
but a secret third thing,
a bark like a retch,
like she's pouring out of herself,
hoarse since she's not used to barking.

I think this poem
is my secret third thing.

it's dark, and I am
slamming my fake-bloody palms

on the chicken-wire lining the edge
of this place, and I don't know
what I want to happen
when you turn around and look.

SPANK BANK

somewhere, still
there's a photo of me
facedown on his bed,
bloated, drunk,
and cooking in his dorm light
like a hot dog.

at 19, there was no time
for composition. it was a risk
to linger, to let something
catch the light. you could see
his shadow staining
my too-blue cotton panties
and a weird edge
where the lace tore in the wash.

his look of admiration
as I posed nearly naked
on the blue-striped sheets,
grease-slick bangs in his eyes
as he knelt between my knees,
tilt-shifting on an ingrown.

it had to do with sex,
but only barely.
it was a friendship, filtered
through the pot-haze
of a tuesday night in Erie,
snow piled too high to walk,

or drive, or think about things
like longevity, or if you maybe
loved each other. same way
I'd rock on his lap play-fighting
in the dead afternoon
and we'd treat it like kids
just fucking around. otherwise
we'd have to get some air.
we'd have to put our coats on.

FRIENDS

in one of my Zoloft dreams
you come riding up to me
on four dead horses.

small and stinking,
your fried-out eyes
pink-rimmed and all pupil,

you jeer me from calf-height
burping halves of jokes that take off
like lit matches past a fan

and when you laugh, I watch
the pink, pustuled bell
dangle at the back of your throat,

some vague suggestion of a heart
or a weak spot, where in a better dream
I'd aim a spell or small, silver arrow,

and you all smell like beer and the same
stale joke you make about Joe pissing the chair
and the chair Joe pissed in

and you all look so much younger
than me and so much worse
than I remember—toasted,
aimless, a handful
of Safeway Beavis and Buttheads
blacked out on the side of the Bayfront Connector

and I could chew you all out
but I'm dreaming,
and the real you has me
blocked on everything.

so I become what I was,
watch you fling slurs around
and dot the curb with puke piles
someone else will clean

and at the end of the night,
I say, "I don't know how
we did this so often,"

and you say, "I don't know
how you stopped."

DM

do you think my writing is good do you take me seriously do you think I'm pretty and does it matter would you ever want to hang out sometime would you take me for drinks would you pay would you make that joke about the money again would you remind me you're everywhere and I'm nowhere and what should I wear when you take off my clothes at the end of the night what will you be expecting who will you be expecting will you be surprised by how femme I still am or were you somehow expecting that too and forgive me I haven't done this before do we kiss or would a kiss give too much away or have I already given too much away am I making this all up don't answer that I hope you put music on I hope you put on some dumb esoteric record that I have never heard of and then whenever I listen to that record I'll think of you the headfuck of you making me feel like a man and a woman at the same time and tell me how is it you do that anyway build me up with worship only to strip it back pin me down grab my wrists make me tell you what I deserve and what i don't and then disappear and leave me an obsessive little loverboy schoolgirl for you two conversations away from dotting i's with little hearts and writing our names together in a book for you, it's so humiliating, just two conversations is all it would take that's how close I am for you that's how close you're getting me you're getting me so fucking close baby and you say how close and I tell you and you snarl and you yank it away and I shudder for hours, keep shuddering, around the space you leave behind.

QUESTIONS

lying in bed on a Sunday afternoon,
I asked if he thought I was funny.

he said, "sure, I guess,
but you're no Robin Williams."

and maybe I shouldn't have given this
so much weight. he could have been confused,
or tired, maybe he just wanted to have sex,
maybe lying there in bed next to me he'd thought
he might roll over and fuck his girlfriend,
like a normal person, and not have to answer
stupid questions, like whether she was funny or not.

but I started to hate him, just a little.
not enough to leave, or to say it, but enough
to start pricking holes in everything,
to let the outside in. I started to want things,
wonder things. I started to have questions.

he did, too. he would come over Fridays
and ask why I never took out my recycling,
when I would buy a TV, why I didn't
have ketchup. he was always hungry,
or tired, or begging me to drink with him
or watch the show he wanted. I messed up
building a bookshelf and he called me stupid.
toward the end, I asked what he even liked about me.
he told me I was "fun." multiple times

he told me this, and he never elaborated,
though we never had fun anymore:
on the beer cruise, I hung out with his brother.
curry night, we bickered over the pan.
we met Jason for dinner, a last-ditch gesture
meant to rekindle things, hoped the three of us would
get along. the whole time, I wanted him gone.

by the time it was ending, and he asked me
what it was he'd done wrong, I couldn't remember,

but I remember the last hug and the way
his body smelled: like an old man, like cardboard,
like something left sitting out too long.

INNER LIFE

dressed and standing
in the self-checkout,
tapping the same few bars
of "Bad to the Bone"
on a frozen pizza,

skipping past
that cloying donation prompt—

you may not like it
but this is what peak performance looks like.

you may not like it,
but before you
stands the avatar
of resilience.

once charged 300 miles
through Pennsyltucky
on a pack of greyhounds
just to fuck fate, the City
of Bridges burnt behind them,

gorged on smiley-face paper
and rode each of the angels
like mechanical bulls.

ate fungus and fucked
the girl at the bottom

of the dark water
who takes your ear
and tells you nothing
exists, there's no one
you can hurt.
on the dismount,
the girl asked
"will we be married?"
and they said no,
and the girl drowned
because she was in love.

you may have heard
that these are unconfirmed reports.

you may have heard
unconfirmed reports
that everything they touch
dies, or at least gets worse.

you should know
they hear them, too,
faintly, during the night
and try to buck them, flailing
in that dark stretch
between light switch and bed
before they can catch.

SUBMISSION GUIDELINES

we are a journal of fiction and poetry.

we are a journal of words.

we are a journal of transgressive, gritty, outsider lit.

we have a name like [Cardinal direction] [U.S. state] Review.

we have a name like Gossamer or TOILET STAIN.

we have a name that uses special unicode characters i am too lazy to type here.

the name of our journal is your favorite color, followed by the name of the street you grew up on, followed by the name of your first grade pet.

the name of our journal is the first three digits of your social security number, followed by the next two digits of your social security number, followed by the final four digits of your social security number (please tell us the name of our journal).

we want your best work.

we want good fiction and good poetry.

we want your heart, your soul, the story only you can tell.

we want words that shock us and confuse us and make us laugh.

we want words that make us feel like shit.

we want words that tell us they love us and then damage us over time through a slow backslide into emotional unavailability that leaves us wondering what we did wrong.

we don't feel interested in words or writing or much of anything anymore, and we want the memory of how that passion felt.

we want you so bad, oh baby, oh baby.

we want your morning breath, your secret car-farts, whatever's growing in the mug you left sitting on your desk.

we want your lunch money. we want your car. we want your girlfriend.

we want the velvety skin on the inside of your wrist.

we want your filmy membranes, your nose drippings and popsicle stains.

we want anything that could be described with the words "fetid" and/or "residue."

we want warm root beer in a glass.

we want a little pomeranian wearing a hat.

we want you to delete that recording of us drunkenly hyperventilating into the toilet at applebee's.

we want you to delete our nudes and our number.

we want pizza.

we want a small harem of hot emo boys to take turns passionately validating our feelings while they massage our neck.

we want our cat to stop sticking his face in our food.

we want an ass tattoo but know deep down it's not actually going to happen.

we want a snack but there's not really anything good in the house so we just keep opening the fridge over and over until we're desperate enough to eat something less thrilling, like a pickle or a slice of cheese.

we want something we cannot articulate and don't know where to find, and we will spend the rest of our lives mauling the people we love in vain trying to claw it out of them. our time on this earth will be marked by a pattern of fleeting, almost manic highs at the prospect of finally filling the swirling chasm inside of us, followed by crushing and prolonged lows at the recurring realization that such a space can never be filled, we will try everything from drugs to sex to angry rampages to asceticism and punishing solitude and continue to come up empty. then, we will meet someone. that someone will remind us of something we'd forgotten. that person will bring us yellow light that we mistake for fulfillment or god. this person will insist on staying, will rebuff any and all fears until we almost trust their permanence. then, one day, we will be lying in bed beside this person and feel heaviness, the imminent ending, and be crushed at how familiar it seems. the next day, they will wake us up before work and kiss our forehead and something about the way they slide out of the bedroom will catch on one of the loose loops closing our heart, send the whole thing exploding open. in the fallout, we'll feel around for that yellow light from before. we'll know it existed, but only like an idea or black-and-white sentence. we won't be able to remember it.

YOUR SECRET
for M.

last year was the first time you cried in front of me.
we were up late drinking when your secret slipped
and you rag-dolled face-first into my lap
like you'd just spit the skeleton out of your body.

I had given up on seeing you open. you were
wound tight in Leo machismo and after years
draining fifths of 151 and breaking our brains
with strips of dark web acid, you'd never once
peeled an inch of it back. now, all of a sudden,
you were wet meat in my arms and everything
hurt. you shook there, tear-stained and raw,
and I felt the air on each newly exposed nerve.
I pulled out your ponytail, combed your curls
with my fingers, watched you go soft and beautiful
between apologies to yourself and your father
and God and the guys on the team
and then to me for the mess you'd been.
you picked your head up and looked at me,
limp and spent in a way that you didn't recognize
and I could tell you found frightening. I didn't
let you know what an honor it was
to see you break. you made me promise not
to tell anyone, and I fell asleep on your couch.

stepping out of the Uber the next morning,
the sky felt so big I should have known

we were standing on a precipice, that those were
the first and last real things we would ever say
to each other and in ten months I wouldn't call you
a friend. instead I spent the whole day trying
to write what would later become this poem,
all red and hot like I'd seen you naked.

wherever you are now, hair gel and ego-slick
in your black leather jacket: I still remember
what you said that night. I'll never tell a soul.

THREESOME

in my dream there was a sex convention, but it was really just a book fair and they were out of wine.

I was nervous.

you were drunk and looking at me like you wanted introductions.

I waved over some guy I'd never seen but apparently knew from somewhere—a dream-friend, I guess, baked into the lore.

you two exchanged the wrong names, so I made you try again, with the right names this time, setting you upright again in front of me like two little toys.

now you say, "hi, my name is," and then say your name.

and now you say it back.

...

I pulled a book off the shelf, convinced it would help me write poetry.

...

a way to loosen things, that's what we needed. we were all so wooden.

like that night with the bright red thong and the playing cards. hearts and diamonds, I took something off; clubs and spades, the two of you. I felt like god each time I peeled one off the deck. the way we'd look at each other, huddled on that little twin bed.

...

I held the book in my hand and an old man walked up to me and said I'd made a good choice and I thought, nevermind, and put the book down.

...

the game was stupid, it was a conceit. we wanted to do it but didn't know how.

...

they stored the booze up on a stage. it was a mad dash, post-apocalyptic, stragglers scrapping over empty-bottle backwash. people passed out with their faces smushed against the thick, red curtains streaked with vomit.

tonight we weren't alone in needing lubrication, some kind of excuse.

I dove for something I thought was whiskey but was just syrup in a fancy bottle.

...

when we'd all drawn enough cards, you made a diagram. an attempt to split the territory. the places we were each allowed to look, to touch. like a team huddled in the locker room, trying to preordain the chaos on the field.

how much of that do you think they really follow, with a packed house, under all of those lights?

I felt hot that night, leaning over your laps in the dark. strung up through the ass in red lace so thin you couldn't breathe on it, not even the pretense of functionality. maybe that was my version of the roaring in the stands, whatever it is that makes you do things you thought you couldn't, like an ill-advised hail-Mary throw.

...

I walked off the stage and came back to our table with nothing.

...

the book said something about intimacy, I think, but in a slant way that felt truer than the things I would typically read. when I saw it I felt excited, and now I regret putting it down.

...

when I saw your faces, I felt embarrassed. I was projecting my own disappointment. after all, I was the only one still sober here, the only one who still needed a boost, or a reason. you looked up at me, expectant. it was so unlike that time before.

...

I was never supposed to be alone with either of you. that's how it was laid out in your diagram: one of you behind me, the other in my mouth. you put me underneath a blanket as a failsafe, no way to tell where one of you ended and where I began, no chance to compete or for your eyes to wander and get hot over the wrong thing, god forbid.

...

for a sex convention, there was very little fucking. I'd expected a whirlwind, to be swept up into some wet, rapturous mob. this was a glorified Scholastic book fair, and we were all just leering at each other.
we wanted it but needed direction.

now you lean forward, and you too.

bend over that convention center table.

...

it was a packed house and nobody came. if you know, you know. you can put in so much effort it's basically impossible. his breath and my breath and yours, every note played straight with no jazz. no one gets off on that kind of control, not even us, not 'til he finished up in the bathroom and left the two of us alone. we made up for lost time, then, our white-hot frustration, the cards fanned out and sliding off the bed.

...

in the dream you tried to kiss me, and I pulled back. the desire was there—this just wasn't the venue. this was academic, and we were animals. designed for something smaller and worse-lit than this, with no fluorescent lights or lanyards. somewhere to sleep.

...

you remember that, right? how the bed seemed so small by the end of it, not meant for three, and you walked out the door, back to your separate room, and we had to pretend it made sense? for his ego, maybe, or some lost cause of feeling like less shitty people.

he was asleep and we were texting each other from behind the two thickest doors in the world, neither of us talking about what had happened, neither of us talking about when my hand grazed your lap and you were wearing those silk, indigo boxers I once saw sitting folded up on your bed and teased you for being a bougie ass.

your mom bought you those. it was weird then that I knew that and weirder now that I remember.

WHALE FALL

the names we called each other stuck
in the teeth of scavengers.

a sleeper shark with "fucktoy" in its mouth,
and "queen," though I never said it to your face,
eating my "suck-your-soul-out eyes"
and how you called them that.

new invertebrates colonizing my holes.

the stick that was up your ass
providing shelter to untold numbers
of organisms who've evolved
to draw nutrients from environments
hostile to most known life-forms.

I could never get your love
and now it's baked into the sediment,
and the shellfish starve
trying to suck it out.

even in death, milking this thing.

I feel something like jealousy.

your fingers rot in my mouth.

THE QUEEN OF DRAG

I wrote a lot of poems about you
and in each one you were sad
and wanting to go somewhere else.

summer at my parents' house
I'd chew on ice cubes for you
over the phone
and you'd tell me
about all the times you thought
you'd gone crazy, too,
so worried about hearing things
you'd start to hear them
crawling in the walls.

Hot Mass, pressed together
in the blackest dark,
our little pills dissolving,
I sang low in your left ear,
huffing your cologne
and you lit up like
the last neon sign for miles.

you almost killed me once
speeding down the wrong side of the bayfront
on a fat hit of DMT.

you were always saying, maybe
I'll go to Japan, or amsterdam

maybe I'll fuck off
and go into the woods,
tell no one where i'm going
and come out
someone new.

you were always saying
we were the same person,
and you were right, so right
that when you left,
I died awhile, reduced
to muffled crying.
water in a small, white cup.

it was the way
you persisted, your loss
vibrating the edges
like a loud fight
in the driveway
outside a party.

and who could blame you?
too cool for the world,
spilling from the walls
of every rented house we drank in,
glowing pink and viscous.

on the timeline I see your eyes
dusted with blue shadow
by the back wall of some club,
and it hurts me in the best way—

your smile a kind of revenge
you were always too pure for,
making all the guys gaunt and monstrous
in your light.

BLOODLETTING ON E. 43RD STREET

I don't think I'll ever stop writing that story of us at the party. you know. the one where I kick my boots off in the mudroom off your kitchen and walk in with a gaping hole in my chest. it's silent, like a dream, like a TV show where the extras don't speak and just mouth words. the crowd parts around me, everyone staring— not just because of the hole, which I am trying and failing to cover with my hands, but some deep-rooted sense that the main character of the scene has finally shown up. I'm dizzy and looking for you. blood is seeping between my fingers, dripping onto the floor, and i'm looking for you. can you come downstairs? are you up there piling coats on the bed? I need you to see this blood trail and make that joke you once made when I spilled the wine. this time, I'll be ready for it. I'll laugh and laugh. it's real this time. I need you. more than the party needs you, than the coats need you, than the bed needs you. it's eating me up inside. I feel the party talking about me even in the silence. they gesture with their eyes, so superior. who cares what they think? this is our moment. you know. the scene in the movie where they say the name of the movie. you're missing it. right now you should have descended the stairs and been so shocked at the sight of me you stumbled and knocked down the suit of armor on the landing. but the stairs are clear and the suit of armor is piled on the bed, weighing the coats down. and where are you? blood is trickling down my shirt. can you come downstairs? can you say your line? the one where your voice quakes at the end and I open my hands and my wound gushes onto my shoes? remember this part? stepping over the fallen armor as I slide my fingertips over the hole, smear them with blood. it's casual. that's the genius of it. I stick my fingers in your mouth and you taste my pain and you're crying, you take it so well, I scoop more of the pain from the hole into your mouth and then I taste some, too. I was ready this time. but you never showed up. you were supposed to taste this with me. you were supposed to feel it. we were supposed to hold each other. this isn't the way I wrote it down and everyone's watching. I feel them judging me with their eyes. I scan the faces for someone I can trust to ask where you went, why you're still up there, why you never looked for me, but it's getting dark and I'm losing a lot of blood—

IT CAN'T ALL BE OVER

we still have
a few good things.

whatever it is
humming in the air
between two people deciding
to tell the truth.

I've never been more naked
than right now, asking how
"over" you think the world really is.

I'm a peeled
fucking lemon.

let's take one minute,
spare a thought
for the grace
it never feels right
to talk about.

late at night,
the hope I unfold
like a blanket,
the stains and the fraying
like something
from a war—but
it isn't a war.
it's the checkout line

on a Friday in 2002
with my mom,
we're in line and she says,
one day you'll be old
and you'll say
"back in my day, we didn't have
hovercraft, we had
to walk everywhere.
we had to sit
in our cars for hours,
stuck on the ground,"
and none of the kids will know
what you're talking about.

WHATEVER

trying to write too many poems at once,
it all nets out to something stupid,
so, whatever. now this looks
how it looks. the room smells
like mixed paints and you can't tell
whose face you're looking at.
Giant Mood. so giant it holds everything
inside it and, in turn, doesn't
mean shit. you've read enough
to know how futile this is, me squinting
and scrambling to name basic shapes
as they dissolve in my hands,
the straw-house urban sprawl
of Real Love dangling ahead
like a carrot. then I sneeze
and forget how to leave my bed.
it's so much work after a while,
calling them houses when I know
I'll spend the next night buried,
hands and knees, scouring
for needles. I'm not doing it
this time. no details. last week
I wished I was dead, but whatever
now, I feel great, but whatever.
whatever whatever whatever,
I can spin the wheel if you want,
and we can pretend whatever
wedge it happens to stop on
was part of the plan all along.

WORD SALAD

The asymptote I'm trying to approach as a poet is this complete one-ness with the reader where they basically just embody my entire consciousness and experience my thoughts, feelings, and memories without any guidance or sensory anchoring whatsoever / when I'm talking to people about that I say I want to "communicate something" but I don't think it's so much that I want to communicate as it is that I don't want to have to communicate

I feel what I can only describe as reverence for the individual nature of my own consciousness and the fact that it contains the only copy of a fucking unfathomably large set of data, and I feel like as a person carrying this consciousness I am completely unequipped to properly pilot it through the world and feed the right things to it / I don't understand how other people seem to take that knowledge so lightly, the knowledge that only they can be themselves and that they've been tasked with doing so for at least the length of an entire human life / how can you feel like you're somehow worthy of that responsibility, of carrying the last/first/only member of a species through a really dangerous landscape and protecting it and properly advocating for it to the people around you / how do you know that someone else wouldn't do a better job / how can you know that you're piloting it as efficiently as possible if nobody else can even fucking see the controls / when I was 19 and 20 I took a lot of acid to try and help myself address these

85

questions but all it did was expose my consciousness to even more experiences specific only to me, further individuating this half-shattered-already, fragile thing that I still have no choice but to carry around / I thought I would have some kind of experience that united me with the universe at large but really it just gave me more reasons to feel alone and paralyzed by the inherent uniqueness of my conscious experience

When I masturbate to a sex fantasy I can't tell if I'm masturbating to the idea of sex with another person or the idea of another person being turned on by me

I vacillate wildly between feeling overwhelmed by how much I seem to feel for/about others and extremely paranoid that I have never actually experienced empathy and the true experience of relating to another human being is pathologically unattainable for me, and what I think is an overwhelming degree of feeling for/about others is really just the absolute baseline level of emotional availability experienced by nearly everyone else

My worst fear is some sort of crushing, all-consuming Judgement that I have always been a bad person and that I am rotten to the core and can never change and don't deserve happiness / I feel fated to experience some expert evaluation by some omniscient character that permanently condemns me as worthless and unlovable and that any evidence to the contrary has been either a result of unconscious manipulation on my part or an utter lie / how fucking Catholic is that

Sometimes I feel uncomfortable around animals because I believe they can see through me, into me, past the entire construction of myself and into some truer, soul-level manifestation of me that I have repressed / I believe that if such a core, soul-type entity exists inside me then it is completely malevolent, in which case everyone's dogs/cats/ goldfish view what I call my Identity as a pathetic and superficial performance of goodness or empathy and view me as someone so good at manipulation that she doesn't even remember these things aren't her true nature / because of this I feel guilty when people like me / because of this I feel deeply ashamed when people don't like me, even if it's on a superficial level or for a more tangible reason / if you're a dog reading this then I want you to know whatever you're seeing when you look through me is completely inaccessible to me and I hope it doesn't disturb you

I can't tell if I should feel comfortable or alienated when someone tells me I think too much / I'm glad not everyone thinks this much and at this resolution but that just places more bullshit on my shoulders doesn't it

Ever since I was a little kid I've wanted to have someone just sit me down and outline my entire psyche for me and tell me exactly why I think/do/wish for the things I do / I was very disappointed the first time I went to therapy and realized they weren't going to do it there, either / poems seem like the closest I can get to that

I used to think if I met someone older or more experienced than me, they would be able to explain me to myself / all that happened was that I got my heart broken a lot and a lot of older men tried to derail my life

I probably don't have to say it at this point, but death scares the fucking shit out of me

It never feels like the appropriate time to ask this: when we grieve are we sad because the person isn't with us anymore or are we sad because we don't know where they went / I know it's a mix of both, obviously, but I guess what I'm asking is do other people feel the second thing or just the first thing / I like to think it'd be easier to accept one's own death and the death of others if it wasn't such fraught, unexplored terrain / it's hard to process someone's absence but also think to yourself "they could be experiencing virtually any number of unfathomable things at this very moment, or perhaps their consciousness just doesn't exist anymore and therefore they aren't experiencing anything at all" / and it's weird how you can spend long periods of time just sort of regarding death in this casual, surface-level way, and then all of a sudden it's in capital letters again and you have to re-learn how to shake it off / if you want to shake it off I don't recommend acid

I want to try something if you don't mind / I'm going to be quiet and you can let me know if you hear me

....

FINAL TRANSMISSION

the closest I get to prayer
is I lie in bed and think of Pittsburgh,
my 7th floor studio with the blank walls
where the super stole my panties from the dryer.

wi-fi siphoned from the nearby Starbucks,
laptop propped on an Amazon box
for a shelf I was too sad to build.

the empty fridge
and the brown, flaccid plant.

it was a brutal year, the kind that later reveals itself
as a way through, some kind of training.
it was shit, and the shit was the point.

you get to say that when it's over—
when you wake up less-broke, sober,
un-inclined to eat pickles over the sink.
when you're no longer drunk in a car
with the man who'll become patient zero
for your sickness, and you his.

I figure you get about a year
between upheavals. precious air
before the old beast returns to feed,
drunk and tripping over itself
like slapstick, and you realize
you aren't as good as you once thought,
same way nothing is.

I know how it looks to reach out now,
so desperately happy.
but I'm not lying, I'm keeping record.
I'm stoned on the beach
watching the sea recede
further and further away
and the kids racing toward it
with buckets.

today, the earthquake
knocked a painting loose
and when it hit the ground
the cat jumped seven feet in the air
and we all laughed so fucking hard.
it actually hurt. I didn't know
I could laugh like that.

Kat Giordano was born in Philadelphia and it's been downhill ever since. They have written two other poetry collections: *Tell Me You've Earned It* (Gob Pile Press, 2023) and *The Poet Confronts Bukowski's Ghost* (Philosophical Idiot, 2013) as well as one novel, *The Fountain* (Thirty West Publishing, 2020). They also run the once-defunct now not-defunct literary website *VANITY* (vanitypress.co) and can be found all over the internet as @giordkat and at katgiordano.com. Kat is very cool. You love them.

"High School Reunion" originally appeared on *Instant Lit*.

"I Am Not A Crook," "Threesome," and "Word Salad" were originally published by *Bullshit Lit*.

"Alone With Everybody" was originally published by *Back Patio Press*.

"A Secret Third Thing" originally appeared in *Bullshit Anthology, Volume 2*.

"Spank Bank" was originally published by *Witch Craft Mag*.

"Bloodletting On E. 43rd Street" was originally published by *Bruiser*.

A selection of these poems were also published as part of a limited-run chapbook with Thirty West Publishing called *Grimming With Brattitude*, released as a companion with pre-orders of *The Fountain*.

Many, many of the original drafts of these poems originally appeared on the Neutral Spaces blog (long may she wave).

Basically, you've seen it all before. Hope that's cool. xo

Still Alive, a novel by LJ Pemberton
Hope and Wild Panic, stories by Sean Ennis
Sleep Decades, stories by Israel A. Bonilla
I Blame Myself But Also You (and Other Stories),
by Spencer Fleury
The Great Atlantic Highway & Other Stories,
by Steve Gergley
First Aid for Choking Victims,
stories by Matthew Zanoni Müller

malarkeybooks.com